Draw Ever

MW01075180
Closer

"Throughout his life, Henri Nouwen read souls and loved people; he hoped, cared, suffered, and showed compassion to all. In *Draw Ever Closer*, we have the opportunity to walk with this spiritual master and receive daily portions of the wisdom that helped him to be such an instrument of peace. Anyone wishing to find new strength or new inspiration to live more passionately or to love more deeply need look no further. The thirty days of this book are for you!"

Rev. Jeffrey Kirby
Author of *Be Not Troubled*

"This devotional is an excellent way for people to get to know Henri Nouwen through his reflections, writing, and spirituality. *Draw Ever Closer* felt like a miniretreat for the soul! This book is a wonderful resource for normal, busy people who are looking for ways to integrate sacred rhythms of work and rest into their lives under Nouwen's loving guidance. Bob Hamma highlights a variety of Nouwen's many works to let the reader really connect with Nouwen on a heart level. This book will be a blessing to people at all stages of the spiritual journey."

Patty Breen
Catholic writer and speaker

"I wholeheartedly second the words of advice found in the beginning of this wonderful book: 'Read slowly. Very slowly. Don't read just to get to the end, but to savor each part of the meditation.' The cadence of each day's prayers calls us to breathe with each line, slowly receiving Henry Nouwen's soul-stirring words. And as we do, we invite in the healing, renewing Spirit of God. All of this happens within the space of mere minutes, making this book both a deeply spiritual and refreshingly practical guide for your journey."

De Yarrison
You Are Made New ministry

Draw Ever Closer

Henri J. M. Nouwen

Edited by Robert M. Hamma

AVE MARIA PRESS AVE Notre Dame, Indiana

Series Editor: John Kirvan

Permissions information and credit lines for all material can be found on p. 93.

_____

Founded in 1865, Ave Maria Press is a ministry of the United States Province of Holy Cross.

www.avemariapress.com

Paperback: ISBN-13 978-1-59471-963-9

E-book: ISBN-13 978-1-59471-964-6

Cover image © vecteezy.com.

Cover and text design by Katherine Robinson.

Printed and bound in the United States of America.

CONTENTS

HENRI NOUWEN

Henri J. M. Nouwen was one of the leading Catholic spiritual writers of the later part of the twentieth century. He was the author of thirty-nine books that sold millions of copies both in the United States and around the world. Nouwen had an exceptional ability to articulate his own inner experience of faith in an unreserved way and was thus able to give voice to the spiritual strivings of not only Catholics but also spiritual seekers of many diverse backgrounds. He once wrote, "By giving words to these intimate experiences I can make my life available to others."[1]

Henri was born on January 24, 1932, in Nijkerk, a city in the Netherlands, and the oldest of four children. His father was a lawyer and his mother a bookkeeper. As early as age six he wanted to be a priest as his uncle Toon was. His grandmother even had little vestments made for him so he could conduct play Masses with his friends.

A gifted student, he attended the Jesuit secondary school in The Hague and then the minor seminary where his uncle was president. He went on to study for six years at the major seminary for the diocese of Utrecht where he was ordained a priest in July 1957.

Always interested in the human experience of faith, Nouwen studied psychology at the Catholic University of Nijmegen. After six years there he received a fellowship to the Religion and Psychiatry Program at the Menninger

Clinic in Topeka, Kansas. The noted psychologist Robert Jonas said of him, "He knew instinctively that he could use his own humanness, his own woundedness in a way that would help ordinary people find a way into grace."[2] Having finished his studies, he spent the most of the next twenty years teaching in America at Notre Dame, Yale, and Harvard, and traveling around the word to speak and lead conferences. Although he relished his work, especially with young people, he was restless about what further direction to take.

During these years he took two sabbaticals to discern where God was calling him. He spent seven months with the Trappists at the Abbey of the Genesee in New York, discerning whether he was called to live a contemplative life. After returning to teaching for a time, he then lived with missionaries in Peru and Bolivia, discerning whether he should work among the poor in the developing world. After six months he returned to the United States and took a part-time teaching position at Harvard Divinity School, which would allow him to return to Latin America for parts of the year.

In 1985 he resigned from Harvard and spent the next year living in at L'Arche, a community in France founded by Jean Vanier where people with differing intellectual abilities live together in community. This was a turning point for Nouwen. When he returned from France he moved into another L'Arche community near Toronto called "Daybreak," where he lived alongside and cared for a young man with profound disabilities named Adam. He spent the last ten years of his life there, caring for Adam and other members of the community as their pastor.

Among the many things that can be said about Henri Nouwen, perhaps one of the most important is that he was a person of prayer who modeled his life on Jesus. Almost all of his books deal with prayer in some way. Because he recognized himself as often distracted, restless, and self-preoccupied, his reflections on prayer speak to the struggles of so many.

Nouwen constantly focused on the gospels and sought to live out the compassion and fidelity of Jesus. In *A Letter of Consolation*, written in memory of his mother, he wrote, "My whole life is centered on the Eucharist. . . . My life must be a continuing proclamation of the death and resurrection of Christ."[3] This is how he understood all of Christian life and in particular his ministry as a priest.

Among the many perspectives from which we can look at the life of Henri Nouwen, perhaps one of the most revealing is through his love of art. Nouwen was profoundly influenced by art and saw it both as a form of prayer and as a text for prayer. In *Behold the Beauty of the Lord* he relates how his parents had purchased a painting of flowers by Marc Chagall long before Chagall was famous. Looking at that painting was a prayerful way for Nouwen to connect with his parents. In the book he reflected on four Russian icons that, he said, "have imprinted themselves so deeply upon my inner life that they appear every time I need comfort or consolation."[4]

Nouwen often referred to Vincent van Gogh in his speaking and writing, and publishers often used van Gogh's art on the covers of Nouwen's books. He once wrote this about van Gogh: "Few writers or painters have influenced me as much. . . . This deeply wounded and gifted Dutchman brought me in touch with my own brokenness and talents in a way that no one else could."[5]

During the last period of his life Nouwen was deeply affected by Rembrandt's painting *The Return of the Prodigal Son*. The image of the embrace between father and son spoke to him at a moment when he was seeking a spiritual home. He wrote, "For so long I had been going from place to place: confronting, beseeching, admonishing, and consoling. Now I desired only to rest safely in a place where I could feel a sense of belonging, a place where I could feel at home."[6]

That place was for him the community at Daybreak. There he learned that he was not only the prodigal son, but also the resentful older brother. And finally he came to the realization that he was being called to transcend the identification with the two sons in the parable and be transformed into their father. "This transformation leads me to the fulfillment of the deepest desire of my restless heart. Because what greater joy can there be for me than to stretch out my tired arms and let my hands rest in a blessing on the shoulders of my homecoming children."[7]

In 1996 Nouwen was invited to participate in the production of a documentary on Rembrandt's painting. On the way to St. Petersburg where the filming was to take place, he stopped in the Netherlands. While there he suffered a massive heart attack and died on September 21, 1996, at the age of sixty-four.

More than twenty years after his death, Nouwen's work continues to inspire readers of all backgrounds and beliefs. His spirit lives on in the work of the Henri Nouwen Society, Henri Nouwen Stichting, the Henri Nouwen Legacy Trust, the Henri J. M. Nouwen Archives and Research Collection, and in all people who embrace the value of communion, community, and ministry, to which he dedicated his life.

HOW TO PRAY
THIS BOOK

The purpose of this book is to open a gate for you, to make accessible the spiritual experience and wisdom of one of our time's most important spiritual teachers, Henri J. M. Nouwen.

This is not a book for mere reading. It invites you to meditate and pray its words on a daily basis over a period of thirty days.

It is a handbook for a spiritual journey.

Before you read the "rules" for taking this spiritual journey, remember that this book is meant to free your spirit, not confine it. If on any day the meditation does not resonate well for you, turn elsewhere to find a passage that seems to best fit the spirit of your day and your soul. Don't hesitate to repeat a day as often as you like until you feel that you have discovered what the Spirit, through the words of the author, has to say to your spirit.

Here are suggestions on one way to use this book as a cornerstone of your prayers.

As Your Day Begins

As the day begins, set aside a quiet moment in a quiet place to read the meditation suggested for the day.

The passage is short. It never runs more than a few hundred words, but it has been carefully selected to give a spiritual focus, a spiritual center to your whole day. It is designed to remind you as another day begins of your own experience at a spiritual level. It is meant to put you in the presence of a spiritual master who is your companion and teacher on this journey. But most of all the purpose of the passage is to remind you that at this moment and at every moment during the day you will be living and acting in the presence of a God who invites you continually but quietly to live in and through him.

A word of advice: Read slowly. Very slowly. The meditation has been broken down into sense lines to help you do just this. Don't read just to get to the end but to savor each part of the meditation. You never know what short phrase, what word, will trigger a response in your spirit. Give the words a chance. After all, you are not just reading this passage; you are praying it. You are establishing a mood of serenity for your whole day. What's the rush?

All Through Your Day

Immediately following the day's reading, you will find a single sentence that we call a mantra.

This phrase is meant as a companion for your spirit as it moves through a busy day. Write it down on a 3" × 5" card or on the appropriate page of your daybook. Look at it as often as you can. Repeat it quietly to yourself, and go on your way.

It is meant not to stop you in your tracks or to distract you from your responsibilities but simply, gently, to remind you of the presence of God and your desire to respond to this presence.

As Your Day Is Ending

This is the time for letting go of the day.

Find a quiet place and quiet your spirit. Breathe deeply. Inhale, exhale—slowly and deliberately, again and again until you feel your body let go of its tension.

Now read the morning prayer slowly, phrase by phrase. You may recognize at once that we have taken one of the most familiar prayers of the Christian tradition and woven into it phrases taken from the meditation with which you began your day and the mantra that has accompanied you all through your day. In this way a simple evening prayer gathers together the spiritual character of the day that is now ending as it began—in the presence of God.

It is a time for summary and closure.

Invite God to embrace you with love and to protect you through the night.

Sleep well.

SOME OTHER WAYS TO USE THIS BOOK

1. Use it any way your spirit suggests. As mentioned earlier, skip a passage that doesn't resonate for you on a given day, or repeat for a second day or even several days a passage whose richness speaks to you. The truths of the spiritual life are not absorbed in a day, or for that matter, in a lifetime. So take your time. Be patient with the Lord. Be patient with yourself.

2. Take two passages or their mantras and "bang" them together. Spend some time discovering how their similarities or differences illumine your path.

3. Start a spiritual journal to record or deepen your experience of this thirty-day journey. Using either the mantra or another phrase from the reading that appeals to you, write a spiritual account of your day, a spiritual reflection. Create your own mediation.

4. Join millions who are seeking to deepen their spiritual life by forming a small group. More and more people are doing just this to support each other in their mutual quest. Meet once a week, or at least every other week, to discuss and pray about one of the meditations. There are many books and guides available to help you make such a group effective.

John Kirvan, Series Editor

THIRTY DAYS WITH

HENRI NOUWEN

DAY 1

My Day Begins

I clearly hear your voice saying,
"Come to me you who labor and are overburdened . . .
for I am gentle and humble in heart,"
and yet I run off in other directions
as if I did not trust you and feel somehow safer
in the company of people whose hearts are divided and
often confused. . . .

Your heart is so full of the desire to love me,
so aflame with a fire to warm me.
You so much want to give me a home,
a sense of belonging, a place to dwell,
a shelter where I feel protected
and a refuge in which I feel safe.
You stand at so many squares and corners of my life
and say with so much tenderness,
"Come and see, come and stay with me.

When you are thirsty, come to me . . .
you who put your trust in me, come and drink.
Come, you who are tired, exhausted,

depressed, discouraged and dispirited.
Come, you who feel pain in your body,
fatigue in your anxious mind
and doubt and anguish in the depth of your heart.
Come and know that I have come to give you
a new heart and a new spirit,
yes, even a new body
in which the struggles of your life
can be seen as signs of beauty and hope."
(*Heart Speaks to Heart*, pp. 22, 25–27)

ALL THROUGH THE DAY

I so want to come to you, O Lord. Help me!

MY DAY IS ENDING

Dear Lord Jesus,
I hear your words,
I want to hear them with my whole being
so that your words can become flesh in me
and form a dwelling place for you.
Help me to close the many doors and windows
of my heart
through which I flee from you
or through which I give entry to words and sounds
coming not from you

but from a raging, screaming world
that wants to pull me away from you. . . .

Please, Lord, keep calling me back to you,
by day and by night, in joy and in sadness,
during moments of success and moments of failure.
Never let me leave you.
I know you walk with me.
Help me walk with you today, tomorrow, and always.
(*Heart Speaks to Heart*, pp. 27, 30)

DAY 2

My Day Begins

Jesus says, "Anyone who loves me
will keep my word
and my Father will love him,
and we shall come to him
and make our home in him."

These words have always impressed me deeply.
I am God's home!
But it had always been very hard
to experience the truth of these words.
Yes, God dwells in my innermost being,
but how could I accept Jesus' call:
"Make your home in me
as I make mine in you"?
The invitation is clear and unambiguous.
To make my home
where God has made his,
this is the great spiritual challenge.

It seemed an impossible task.
With my thoughts, feelings,
emotions, and passions,

I was constantly away
from the place where God had chosen
to make his home.
Coming home and staying there
where God dwells,
listening to the voice of truth and love,
that was, indeed, the journey I most feared
because I knew that God was a jealous lover
who wanted every part of me,
all the time.
When would I be ready to accept that kind of love?
God himself showed me the way.
(*The Return of the Prodigal Son,* pp. 16–17)

A LL T HROUGH THE D AY

You are my home. I dwell in you.

M Y D AY I S E NDING

Lord Jesus,
as this day comes to an end,
let me be at home in you
as you are at home in me.
This day, like every day,
I have been busy about many things,
attending to my many responsibilities and obligations.

I have been rushing around, worrying about what
comes next,
forgetting the one thing that is necessary—
your sustaining presence.
Remind me that, if I want to find you
in the midst of my haste and activity,
I must first remember that you are already here
within me.
Thank you, Lord, for your loving patience
and your tender care.

DAY 3

....

MY DAY BEGINS

Augustine said: "My soul is restless
until it rests in you, O God,"
but when I examine
the tortuous story of our own salvation,
I see not only
that we are yearning to belong to God,
but that God is yearning to belong to us.

It seems as if God is crying out to us,
"My heart is restless until I may rest in you,
my beloved creation."
From Adam and Eve to Abraham and Sarah,
from Abraham and Sarah to David and Bathsheba
to Jesus and ever since,
God cries out to be received by his own.

"I created you,
I gave you all my love,
I guided you, offered you my support,
promised you the fulfillment of your hearts' desires:
where are you, where is your response,
where is your love?

What else must I do to make you love me?
I won't give up. I will keep trying.
One day you will discover
how I long for your love!"
(*With Burning Hearts*, pp. 69–70)

ALL THROUGH THE DAY

My restless heart longs for you.

MY DAY IS ENDING

My soul is indeed restless, O Lord,
yearning for a peace that only you can give.
You are, in truth, my heart's deepest desire,
though I continually seek fulfillment elsewhere.
Let me hear your voice crying out to me,
In each act of kindness,
each caring touch,
each personal word
that I have received or exchanged with others today.
Let them not be merely passing moments
that get me through the day,
but invitations to make me love you.
Help me remember how much you long for my love.
Let me never forget that my longing for you
is but a shadow of your longing for me.

DAY 4

MY DAY BEGINS

Jesus is a very interesting person.
His words are full of wisdom.
His presence is heartwarming.
His gentleness and kindness are deeply moving.
His message is very challenging.
But do we invite him into our home?
Do we want him to come to know us
behind the walls of our most intimate life?
Do we want to introduce him
to all the people we live with?
Do we want him to see us in our everyday lives?
Do we want him to touch us
where we are most vulnerable?
Do we want him to enter
into the back rooms of our homes,
rooms that we ourselves
prefer to keep safely locked?
Do we truly want him
to stay with us when it is nearly evening
and the day is almost over? . . .

Jesus reveals himself as the Good Shepherd
who knows us intimately and loves us.
But do we want to be known by him?
Do we want him to walk freely
in every room of our inner lives?
Do we want him to see our bad side
as well as our good,
our shadow as well as our light?
Or do we prefer him to go on
without entering our home?
In the end the question is:
"Do we really trust him
and entrust every part of ourselves to him?"
(*With Burning Hearts*, pp. 57–58)

ALL THROUGH THE DAY

Jesus, gentle shepherd, you know me and love me.

MY DAY IS ENDING

It is true, Lord,
that sometimes I keep you at a distance.
There are parts of me that I do not want to show you,
relationships that I want to keep separate from you,
ambitions and goals into which I don't want to invite you.
How foolish I am, how childish,

to think that you do not already know
about everything I cling to,
everything I hide,
everything I want.

Yet your love embraces every part of me,
seeks to bring to the light everything that I cover up.
Only you can heal all that is broken
and bring to light all that is in darkness.
Help me to let you in.

DAY 5

My Day Begins

For many years I tried to get a glimpse of God
by looking at the varieties of human experience:
loneliness and love, sorrow and joy,
resentment and gratitude, war and peace.
I sought to understand the ups and downs of the
human soul,
to discern there the hunger and thirst
that only a God whose name is love could satisfy. . . .
I tried constantly to point beyond
the mortal quality of our existence
to a presence larger, deeper,
wider, more beautiful than we can imagine,
and to speak about that presence
as a presence that can already now
be seen, heard, and touched
by those who are willing to believe.

However, during my time here at Daybreak
I have been led to an inner place
where I had not been before.
It is the place within me

where God has chosen to dwell.
It is the place where I am held safe
in the embrace of an all-loving Father
who calls me by name and says,
"You are my beloved son, on you my favor rests."
It is the place where I can taste
the joy and the peace that are not of this world.
(*The Return of the Prodigal Son*, p. 16)

All Through the Day

"You are my beloved child, my favor rests on you."

My Day Is Ending

All loving Father,
today I have glimpsed you
in the faces of the people I've seen,
caught the sound of your voice
in their laughter and cries of pain,
touched your hands
in the warmth or coldness of their hands.
I have sought you in the ups and downs of my heart,
in loneliness and love, in sorrow and joy,
in the midst of my inner turmoil
and in quiet moments of peace.
And yet my soul is still restless,

my heart still longs for more.
Let me rest now in the quiet of this night
and remember that as much as I seek you,
you are seeking me even more
and hold me always in your heart
as your beloved child.

DAY 6

My Day Begins

At issue here is the question,
"To whom do I belong?
To God or to the world?"
Many of my daily preoccupations suggest
that I belong more to the world than to God.
A little criticism makes me angry,
and a little rejection makes me depressed.
A little praise raises my spirits,
and a little success excites me.
It takes very little to raise me up
or thrust me down.

Often I am like a small boat on the ocean,
completely at the mercy of its waves.
All the time and energy I spend
in keeping some kind of balance
and preventing myself
from being tipped over and drowning
shows me that my life is
mostly a struggle for survival:
not a holy struggle,

but an anxious struggle
resulting from the mistaken idea
that it is the world that defines me.

As long as I keep running about asking,
"Do you love me? Do you really love me?"
I give all power to the voices of the world
and put myself in bondage
because the world is filled with "ifs."
The world says, "Yes, I love you if . . ."
(*The Life of the Beloved*, p. 42)

All Through the Day

"I have called you by name, you are mine."

My Day Is Ending

Dear Lord,
As this day comes to an end,
I offer you my fragile, fickle heart.
You know well my fears and insecurities,
my need for affirmation and praise,
my grasping and clinging ways.
I know you are there
below the surface of my turbulent existence.
Remind me that unlike the world's love,

your love is unconditional.
Keep me tethered to you
do not let me go.
You are my anchor, my security.

DAY 7

My Day Begins

I am the prodigal son
every time I search for unconditional love
where it cannot be found.
Why do I keep ignoring the place of true love
and persist in looking for it elsewhere?
Why do I keep leaving home
where I am called to be a child of God,
the beloved of my Father?

I am constantly surprised
by how I keep taking the gifts that God has given me—
my health, my intellectual and emotional gifts—
and keep using them to impress people,
receive affirmations and praise,
and compete for rewards,
instead of developing them for the glory of God.
Yes, I often carry them off to a "distant country"
and put them in the service of an exploiting world
that does not know their true value.
It's almost as if I want to prove to myself
and to my world

that I do not need God's love,
that I can make a life on my own,
that I want to be fully independent.

Beneath it all is the great rebellion,
the radical "No" to the Father's love. . . .
The prodigal son's no
reflects Adam's original rebellion:
his rejection of the God
in whose love we are created
and by whose love we are sustained.
(*The Life of the Beloved*, p. 43)

A LL   T HROUGH   THE   D AY

Come home to me.

M Y   D AY   I S   E NDING

Dear God,
you have given me so much.
Your gifts to me are countless.
How have I used these gifts today?

How has my presence
affected the people I have encountered today?
Have I been trying to impress them,
to make them notice me

and think well of me?
Or have I rather been focused on them,
trying to reflect your care,
your compassion,
your mercy?

Am I trying to prove something to others?
Am I letting myself be carried away
by vain hopes of adulation?
Or am I angry and resentful
at not being appreciated,
not being regarded
as highly as someone else?

Lord, you have probed me
and you know me.
Before a thought enters my mind
you know it.
There is nowhere I can go
that is beyond the reach of your love.
Do not let me wander far from you.
Bring me home
to your loving embrace.

DAY 8

My Day Begins

How can we live in the midst of a world
marked by fear, hatred, and violence,
and not be destroyed by it?
When Jesus prays to his Father for his disciples
he responds to this question by saying,
"I am not asking you to remove them from the world
but to protect them from the Evil One.
They do not belong to the world
any more than I belong to the world" (Jn 17:15–16).

To live in the world without belonging to the world
summarizes the essence of the spiritual life.
The spiritual life keeps us aware that our true house
is not the house of fear,
in which the powers of hatred and violence rule,
but the house of love, where God resides.
Hardly a day passes in our lives
without our experience of inner or outer fears,
anxieties, apprehensions, and preoccupations.
These dark powers have pervaded
every part of our world

to such a degree that we can never fully escape them.
Still it is possible not to belong to these powers,
not to build our dwelling place among them,
but to choose the house of love as our home.

This choice is made not just once and for all
but by living a spiritual life,
praying at all times
and thus breathing God's breath.
Through the spiritual life we gradually move
from the house of fear to the house of love.
(*Behold the Beauty of the Lord*, pp. 30–31)

ALL THROUGH THE DAY

Do not fear, I am with you.

MY DAY IS ENDING

Jesus,
I remember your words about the two houses,
one built on sand that falls when the storm comes,
and one built on rock that stands strong.
I think my house is somewhere in between.
Some of the things that I do strengthen its foundation,
some weaken it.
I know that the real threats to my house

are not hatred, violence, or some great sin
that is probably too bold for me to commit.
The real danger for me
is the corrosive power of fear.

This fear has many ways of taking hold of me.
It takes the form of anxieties,
apprehensions, and preoccupations.
It paralyzes me and keeps me from trusting,
from living in the present moment,
from forgiving and letting go.

Remind me Lord,
that the lure of the world
is not so much the power of wealth,
or fame, or success.
The danger is letting fear have its sway,
allowing anxiety, apprehension, and preoccupation
to corrode the foundation of my house.
Help me, Lord,
to make my house a house of love,
and not a house of fear.

DAY 9

M Y   D A Y   B E G I N S

Often the burdens of our past
seem too heavy for us to carry alone.
Shame and guilt make us hide part of ourselves
and thus make us live half lives.
We truly need each other to claim all of our lives
and to live them to the fullest.
We need each other to move beyond
our guilt and shame
and to become grateful,
not just for our successes and accomplishments
but also for our failures and shortcomings.

We need to be able to let our tears flow freely,
tears of sorrow as well as tears of joy,
tears that are as rain on dry ground.
As we thus lift our lives for each other,
we can truly say: "To life,"
because all we have lived now
becomes the fertile soil for the future. . . .
It means that we take all we have ever lived
and bring it to the present moment

as a gift for others, a gift to celebrate.
(*Can You Drink the Cup?* pp. 79–80)

ALL THROUGH THE DAY

Make my life a gift to others.

MY DAY IS ENDING

O Lord,
Most of the time
I am willing to look at my life and say,
"I am grateful for the good things that brought me to
this place."
But I need your help
to hold my life in my hands
and to lift up the cup of my life and say,
"I am grateful for all that has happened to me
and led me to this moment."

Give me the gratitude to embrace all of my past
so that I can make my life a true gift for others.
Let this gratitude erase
bitterness, resentments, regret, and revenge
as well as all jealousies and rivalries.
Let it transform the past
into a fruitful gift for the future.

Help me, Lord,
to embrace all of my life
and make my life, all of it,
into a life that gives life.

DAY 10

My Day Begins

Our life is a short time in expectation,
a time in which sadness and joy kiss each other at
every moment.
There is a quality of sadness that pervades all the
moments of our life.
It seems that there is no such thing as clear-cut
pure joy,
but that even in the most happy moments
of our existence
we sense a tinge of sadness.
In every satisfaction, there is an awareness
of its limitations.
In every success, there is the fear of jealousy.
Behind every smile, there is a tear.
In every embrace, there is loneliness.
In every friendship, distance.
And in all forms of light,
there is the knowledge of surrounding darkness.

Joy and sadness are as close to each other
as the splendid colored leaves of a New England fall
to the soberness of the barren trees.

When you touch the hand of a returning friend,
you already know that he will have to leave you again.
When you are moved by the quiet vastness of a
sun-covered ocean,
you miss the friend who cannot see the same.
Joy and sadness are born at the same time,
both arising from such deep places in your heart
that you can't find words
to capture your complex emotions.
(*Out of Solitude,* pp. 53–54)

A LL T HROUGH THE D AY

I will hold joy and sadness gently, together.

M Y D AY I S E NDING

Dear Jesus,
sometimes there are no words
to express what I am feeling
when joy is tinged with sadness,
and sadness mingled with joy.
It is a deep truth
that can move me to tears,
or can make me want to turn away.

Lord Jesus,
you are like us in all things but sin,
so you knew well this joy, this sadness.
You laughed, you wept.
You celebrated life, you cried at its passing.
And when it came time
to take hold of your life and give it away
for our sake, for me,
you said yes to your Father,
yes to all that you had lived.

You breathed out your last,
giving us your Spirit
whose presence is found
where joy and sadness meet.
You commended your life into the Father's hands—
in pain, yet with joy.
Help me, this night, to do the same.

DAY 11

....

Resentment is one of the most destructive forces
in our lives.
It is cold anger that has settled
into the core of our being
and hardened our hearts.
Resentment can become a way of life
that so pervades our words and actions
that we no longer recognize it as such. . . .
Resentment is such an obvious response
to our many losses. . . .

Still the Eucharist presents another option.
It is the possibility to choose,
not resentment, but gratitude.
Mourning our losses is the first step
away from resentment and toward gratitude.
The tears of our grief
can soften our hardened hearts
and open us to the possibility to say "thanks."
The word "Eucharist" means literally
"act of thanksgiving."
To celebrate the Eucharist

and to live a Eucharistic life
has everything to do with gratitude.
Living Eucharistically
is living life as a gift,
a gift for which one is grateful.
(*With Burning Hearts*, pp. 29–30)

All Through the Day

I will choose gratitude, not resentment.

My Day Is Ending

Gracious God,
as this day comes to an end,
I pause to remember the people
I have encountered today.
Each one, by name.

I give thanks to you, my God,
for placing them in my life.
Let me see them as you do,
with loving, patient care.
Help me to appreciate them,
to focus on their goodness
rather than their foibles or failings.
Let me remember that I too

have foibles and failings
and that you have endless patience with me.

I call some others to mind as well,
those who bother me or have hurt me.
It saddens me to remember these painful moments
yet I want to release them.
Help me let go of the hurts,
for it does me no good to hold onto them.
Let me not judge, lest I be judged.
Let me forgive, as you have forgiven me.

Cleanse me of resentment.
Free my heart from the burdens of the past.
Fill me with gratitude for all that I have received.

DAY 12

MY DAY BEGINS

Is God present or is he absent?
Maybe we can say now
that in the center of our sadness for his absence
we can find the first signs of his presence.
And that in the middle of our longings
we discover the footprints
of the one who has created them.
It is in the faithful waiting for the loved one
that we know how much he has filled our lives already.
Just as the love of a mother for her son
can grow while she is waiting for his return,
and just as lovers can rediscover each other
during long periods of absence,
so also our intimate relationship with God
can become deeper and more mature
while we wait patiently in expectation for his return.
(*Out of Solitude*, p. 61)

ALL THROUGH THE DAY

Show me the traces of your presence
in the midst of my longing.

MY DAY IS ENDING

Teach me patience, O Lord.
I so want to feel your presence with me,
to know you are near.
But when I don't hear your voice
or sense the movement of your Spirit within me,
I become impatient, anxious, and fearful.
I forget the times when you have been so near to me.
I sometimes even doubt if those times were real.
I am like a little child
crying for its mother in the night.

As this day ends,
let me remember a moment
when your presence was very real to me.
Perhaps it was a moment of joy
a time when I was filled with gratitude
for the gifts of life and love.
Perhaps it was a moment of sorrow
when in the midst of my tears
your touch offered comfort and hope.
Perhaps it was a moment of wonder
when the beauty and mystery of creation
filled me with awe.

Truly Lord, you have gifted me
with many such moments.
Yet I so easily forget.
Keep these close to me now
when your presence seems elusive.
Let me wait peacefully,
confident that you are always near
even if I do not see you.

DAY 13

MY DAY BEGINS

Praying is no easy matter.
It demands a relationship in which you allow
someone other than yourself to enter
into the very center of your person,
to see what you would rather leave in darkness,
and to touch there
what you would rather leave untouched.

Why would you really want to do that?
Perhaps you would let the other cross your threshold
to see something or to touch something,
but to allow the other into that place
where your most intimate life is shaped—
that is dangerous and calls for defense.
The resistance to praying
is like the resistance of a tightly clenched fist. . . .
When you want to pray, then,
the first question is:
How do I open my closed hands? . . .

Don't be afraid of the One
who wants to enter your most intimate space

and invites you to let go of
what you are clinging to so anxiously.
Each time you dare to let go
and to surrender one of those many fears,
your hand opens a little
and your palms spread out in a gesture of receiving.
(*With Open Hands*, pp. 19–20, 24–25)

All Through the Day

I stand before you with empty, open hands.

My Day Is Ending

Dear God,
I am so afraid to open my clenched fists!
Who will I be when I have nothing to hold on to?
Who will I be when I stand before you
with empty hands?
Please help me to gradually open my hands
to discover that I am not my own,
but what you want to give me.
And what you want to give me is love—
unconditional, everlasting love.
(*With Open Hands*, p. 27)

DAY 14

My Day Begins

Today, noise is the normal fare . . .
and silence has become the disturbance. . . .
But more difficult than getting rid of exterior noises
is the achievement of inner silence,
a silence of the heart. . . .

It is hardly surprising, then, that when we shut off all
the daily racket,
a new inner noise can often be heard,
rising from all those chaotic feelings
and screaming for attention.
Entering into a quiet room doesn't automatically bring
us inner silence.
When there is no one to talk to or to listen to,
an interior discussion may start up—
often noisier than the noise we just escaped.
Many unsolved problems demand attention;
one care forces itself upon the other;
one complaint rivals the next,
all pleading for a hearing.
Sometimes we are left powerless

in the face of the many twisted sentiments
we cannot untangle. . . .

The question is . . .
whether we can stand to be alone from time to time,
shut our eyes,
gently push aside all the assorted noises,
and sit calmly and quietly. . . .
But whenever you do come upon this silence,
it seems as though you have received a gift,
one which is "promising" in the true sense of the word.
The promise of this silence is that new life can be born.
It is this silence which is the silence
of peace and prayer
because it brings you back
to the One who is leading you.
(*With Open Hands*, pp. 33, 36, 37, 38, 43)

A L L   T H R O U G H   T H E   D A Y

I will gently push aside all the assorted noises
and sit calmly and quietly.

MY DAY IS ENDING

Dear God,
Speak gently in my silence.
When the loud outer noises of my surroundings
and the loud inner noises of my fears
keep pulling me away from you,
help me to trust that you are still there
even when I am unable to hear you.
Give me ears to listen
to your small, soft voice saying:
"Come to me, you who are overburdened,
and I will give you rest. . . .
for I am gentle and humble of heart."
Let that loving voice be my guide.
Amen.
(*With Open Hands*, p. 45)

DAY 15

MY DAY BEGINS

Deep silence leads us to realize that prayer is,
above all, acceptance.
When we pray, we are standing with our hands open to
the world.
We know that God will become known to us
in the nature around us,
in people we meet,
and in situations we run into.
We trust that the world holds God's secret within
and we expect that secret to be shown to us.
Prayer creates that openness in which
God is given to us.
Indeed, God wants to be admitted
into the human heart,
received with open hands,
and loved with the same love
with which we have been created.
This openness, however, does not come
simply of itself.
It requires a confession that you are limited,
dependent, weak, and even sinful.

Whenever you pray,
you profess that you are not God
nor do you want to be God,
that you haven't reached your goal yet,
and that you never will reach it in this life,
and that you must constantly stretch out your hands
and wait for the gift of life.
This attitude is difficult because
it makes you vulnerable.
(*With Open Hands*, pp. 47–48)

ALL THROUGH THE DAY

I will let you enter into my heart.

MY DAY IS ENDING

Lord, as this day ends
I open my hands to you
and to the world that you have given me to dwell in.
I recall the people who have crossed my path today.
I know that each one of them is loved by you
in the same way as I am.
I recall to the beauty of this world
in the glimpses of your creation I have seen today
and in the moments of kindness I have witnessed.

I believe, O God,
that this world holds your secret within it
and that I can only discover its hidden depths
by opening myself to you, more and more.
You have created in me, O God,
a space that only you can fill.
I know that the more I open myself to you,
the more you can enter into that space
and show me the depth and the breadth
of your love and presence
in me and in the world.
Let me begin to see that hidden wisdom
that dwells in the secret depths of my heart
and in the heart of your creation.

DAY 16

MY DAY BEGINS

In solitude we can slowly unmask
the illusion of our possessiveness
and discover in the center of our own self
that we are not what we can conquer,
but what is given to us.
In solitude we can listen to the voice of him
who spoke to us before we could speak a word,
who healed us
before we could make any gesture to help,
who set us free long before we could free others,
and who loved us
long before we could give love to anyone.

It is in this solitude that we discover
that being is more important than having,
and that we are worth more
than the result of our efforts.
In solitude we discover
that our life is not a possession to be defended,
but a gift to be shared.

It is there that we recognize that the healing words that
we speak
are not just our own, but are given to us;
that the love we can express is part of a greater love;
and that the new life that we bring forth
is not a property to cling to,
but a gift to be received.
In solitude we become aware
that our worth is not the same as our usefulness.
(*Out of Solitude*, pp. 25–26)

All Through the Day

Let me not be afraid of solitude.

My Day Is Ending

Dear God,
I am holding on to so many things
that fill me with worry and anxiety.
When I seek a place of solitude within,
I find there a hundred concerns
about the day just passed
and what the future will bring.
These worries seem to possess me.
They deceive me into believing

that I can overcome them on my own
if I just work harder or plan better.

Still these voices.
Calm my troubled heart.
Remind me that you are near—
the stillness beneath the turmoil,
the center of my very self.
Let me rest there,
and let me rise to a new day
in which I can receive what you give me
and love from your love
that dwells within me.

DAY 17

··

Perhaps the challenge of the gospel
lies precisely in the invitation to accept a gift
for which we can give nothing in return.
For the gift is the life-breath of God,
the Spirit poured out on us through Jesus Christ.
This life-breath frees us from fear and gives us new
room to live.
Those who live prayerfully are constantly ready
to receive the breath of God
and to let their lives be renewed and expanded.
Those who never pray, on the contrary, are like
children with asthma:
because they are short of breath,
the whole world shrivels up before them.
They creep into a corner gasping for air
and are virtually in agony.

But those who do pray open themselves to God
and can breathe freely again.
They stand upright, stretch out their hands,
and come out of their corner,
free to move about without fear.

When we live from God's breath we recognize with joy
that the same breath that keeps us alive
is also the source of life for our brothers and sisters.
This realization makes our fear of the other disappear,
our weapons fall away, and brings a smile to our lips.
When we recognize the breath of God in others,
we can let them enter our lives
and receive the gifts they offer us.
(*With Open Hands*, pp. 54–55)

ALL THROUGH THE DAY

Receive the breath of God.

MY DAY IS ENDING

Gentle Spirit, Breath of Life,
you are always new, always different.
As I breathe in, let me recognize
that you are the very source of my life.
As I breathe out,
help me remember that I am yours.
As I breathe in, I accept all you have given me.
As I breathe out, I return it to you with thanks.
I do not know what you have in store for me,
but I trust that whatever the future may hold
you will be there.

As the journey of my life unfolds
you call me to give myself in ever new ways—
new challenges, new opportunities,
new people, new places
all offer me new opportunities to encounter you.
And as each day unfolds
there are still all of the responsibilities
and commitments
that have shaped my life thus far.

Come, O Spirit of Life,
and weave together the many strands of my life,
past, present, and to come,
into a tapestry of praise and thanks
for all that has been and all that will be.

DAY 18

....

The important thing about prayer
is not whether it is classified as petition, thanksgiving,
or praise,
but whether it is a prayer of hope or of little faith.
The prayer of little faith makes us cling
to the concrete circumstances of the present situation
in order to win a certain security.
The prayer of little faith is filled with wishes
which beg for immediate fulfillment.
This kind of prayer has a Santa Claus naiveté about it
and wants the direct satisfaction of very specific
wishes and desires.
When this prayer is not heard . . .
when we don't get the presents we wanted,
there is disappointment,
even hard feelings and bitterness.

When we live with hope
we do not get tangled up with concerns
for how our wishes will be fulfilled.
So, too, our prayers are not directed toward the gift,

but toward the one who gives it.
Our prayers might still contain just as many desires,
but ultimately it is not a question of having a wish
come true
but of expressing an unlimited faith
in the giver of all good things.
You wish that . . . but you hope in . . .
(*With Open Hands*, pp. 68–73)

A LL T HROUGH THE D AY

I hope in you, my God.

M Y D AY I S E NDING

Dear God,
I am full of wishes,
full of desires,
full of expectations.
Some of them may be realized, many may not,
but in the midst of all my satisfactions and
disappointments,
I hope in you.

I know that you will never leave me alone
and will fulfill your divine promises.
Even when it seems that things are not going my way,

I know that they are going your way
and that, in the end, your way is the best way for me.
O Lord, strengthen my hope,
especially when my many wishes are not fulfilled.
Let me never forget that your name is Love.
Amen.
(*With Open Hands*, p. 78)

DAY 19

My Day Begins

Prayer has meaning only if it is necessary
and indispensable.
Prayer is prayer only when we can say
that without it, we cannot live.
How can this be true or be made true?
The word that brings us closest to an answer
to this question
is the word "compassion." . . .

When you pray, you discover
not only yourself and God,
but also your neighbor.
For in prayer, you profess not only that
people are people
and God is God,
but also that your neighbor is your sister or brother
living alongside you.
For the same conversion that brings you
to the painful acknowledgment of your wounded
human nature
also brings you to the joyful recognition

that you are not alone,
but that being human means being together. . . .
At the moment that you fully realize
that the God who loves you unconditionally
loves all your fellow human beings with the same love,
a new way of living opens itself to you.
For you come to see with new eyes
those who live beside you in this world.
(*With Open Hands*, pp. 85, 91, 94)

ALL THROUGH THE DAY

Your love embraces all, unconditionally.

MY DAY IS ENDING

Dear God,
As you draw me ever deeper into your heart,
I discover that my companions on the journey are
women and men
loved by you as fully and as intimately as I am.
In your compassionate heart, there is a place
for all of them.
No one is excluded.
Give me a share in your compassion, dear God,
so that your unlimited love may become visible

in the way I love my brothers and sisters.

Amen.

(*With Open Hands*, p. 97)

DAY 20

My Day Begins

Out of his solitude
Jesus reached out his caring hand
to the people in need.
In the lonely place his care grew strong and mature.
And from there he entered into a healing closeness
with his fellow human beings.

Jesus indeed cared.
Being pragmatists we say: "That is obvious:
he fed the hungry, made the blind see,
the deaf hear, the crippled walk and the dead live.
He indeed cared."
But by being surprised
by all the remarkable things he did,
we forget that Jesus did not give food to the many
without having received some loaves and fishes
from a stranger in the crowd;
that he did not return the boy of Nain
to his widowed mother
without having felt her sorrow;
that he did not raise Lazarus from the grave

without tears and a sigh of distress
that came straight from the heart.

What we see, and like to see, is cure and change.
But what we do not see and do not want to see is care:
the participation in the pain,
the solidarity in suffering,
the sharing in the experience of brokenness.
And still, cure without care is as dehumanizing
as a gift given with a cold heart.
(*Out of Solitude*, pp. 35–36)

All Through the Day

Let me see the brokenness, pain, and suffering
around me.

My Day Is Ending

Lord, as this day ends
I bring to mind the many ways
I have been called to care for others today.
In the midst of all I have to do,
sometimes I just move from one task to the next
without really thinking about the other person.
Help me to pause now and reflect
on these many people and the needs they have.

Some needs may seem trivial and routine,
but their needs are still important to them.

I recall your words that anyone who gives
a drink of water to the thirsty gives it to you.
Just a little thing to do, yet full of meaning.
Let me to be more mindful as I try to care for others.
Help me to enter into their needs
and recognize that their needs are like mine,
and to see you in those for whom I care.
I too have been cared for by others today.
Thank you for their kindness
and for the way you care for me through them.

DAY 21

....

What does it mean to live in the world
with a truly compassionate heart,
a heart that remains open
to all people at all times?
It is very important to realize that compassion
is more than sympathy or empathy.
When we are asked to listen
to the pains of people
and empathize with their suffering,
we soon reach our emotional limits.
We can listen only for a short time
and only to a few people.

In our society we are bombarded with so much "news"
about human misery
that our hearts easily get numbed
simply because of the overload.
But God's compassionate heart
does not have limits.
God's heart is greater, infinitely greater,
than the human heart.
It is that divine heart

that God wants to give to us
so that we can love all people
without burning out or becoming numb.
(*Here and Now*, pp. 109–110)

ALL THROUGH THE DAY

A pure heart create for me, O God.

MY DAY IS ENDING

Lord, I don't know
if I can keep my heart open
to all people, at all times.
When I hear of the atrocities of war,
refugees living in squalid conditions,
famine, disease, homelessness, and poverty,
I am overwhelmed.
I want to turn away and shut it all out.
Even with family and friends
I weary of hearing the same complaints,
over and over.
I don't know how to hold all this suffering in my heart.

Dear Lord,
I know that your heart is not like mine.
Your heart is greater, limitless,

able to welcome the pain and suffering
of every one of your children.
Just as you know me and love me
in the same way you know and love
each man, each woman, each child
who is suffering at this moment.

Teach me how to look in the eyes
of just one suffering person
and recognize
the depth and breadth of his or her pain.
Teach me to do this with one person,
then another, and then another.
And show me how to do something,
one thing at a time.
Soften my heart, little by little.
Let me enter gradually
into the boundless compassion of your heart.

DAY 22

MY DAY BEGINS

Shortly after hearing the voice
calling him the Beloved,
and soon after rejecting Satan's voice
daring him to prove to the world
that he is worth being loved,
[Jesus] begins his public ministry.
One of his first steps is to call disciples
to follow him and share in his ministry.

Then Jesus goes up on the mountain,
gathers his disciples around him, and says:
"How blessed are the poor, the gentle,
those who mourn,
those who hunger and thirst for righteousness,
the merciful,
the pure of heart,
the peacemakers,
and those who are persecuted
in the cause of uprightness."
These words present a portrait of the child of God.
It is a self-portrait of Jesus, the Beloved Son.

It is also a portrait of me as I must be.
(*The Life of the Beloved*, p. 54)

ALL THROUGH THE DAY

May my life reflect yours, O Lord.

MY DAY IS ENDING

As this day ends
I will focus on the Beatitudes
as a portrait of the child of God
and recall the words from the Letter to the Ephesians:
"You are God's work of art."

This day, like every day,
I have had the opportunity to allow you,
Lord Jesus, to add a few more brushstrokes
to the portrait you are painting of me,
as a child of your Father.
You are a patient artist,
waiting for me to let you apply
the paints you wish to use.
These are not the colors or brushstrokes
of success, accomplishment,
or recognition from others.

You prefer instead to use
shades of mercy, gentleness, and purity of heart.

What kind of paints have I given you
to work with today?
Have I acted gently and shown mercy to my family
and friends?
Have I shown compassion toward the poor
and recognized my own poverty?
Have I hungered for righteousness
or thirsted for justice?
Have I allowed the grief of others to affect me?

Purify my heart, O Lord,
so that I can let you paint the portrait of me
that you wish to create.
Help me to stop trying to craft an image of myself
that I think the world wants to see,
that will prove that I am worthy of being loved.
Help me to let you paint an image of me
as you know me, truly, fully.
Let my life be a reflection of you.

DAY 23

My Day Begins

The compassionate life
is the life of downward mobility!
In a society where upward mobility is the norm,
downward mobility is not only discouraged
but even considered unwise, unhealthy,
and downright stupid. . . .
My whole life I have been surrounded
by well-meaning encouragement to go "higher up,"
and the most used argument was:
"You can do so much good there, for so many people."
But these voices calling me to upward mobility
were completely absent from the Gospel.

Jesus says: "Anyone who loves his life loses it;
anyone who hates his life in this world
will keep it for eternal life" (Jn 20:25).
He also says: "Unless you become like little children
you will never enter the kingdom of heaven" (Mt 18:3).
This is the way of downward mobility,
the descending way of Jesus.
It is the way toward the poor, the suffering,
the marginal,

the prisoners, the lonely, the hungry,
the dying, the tortured, the homeless—
toward all who ask for compassion.
What do they have to offer?
Not success, popularity, or power,
but the joy and peace of the children of God.
(*Here and Now*, pp. 100–101)

A LL T HROUGH THE D AY

The last shall be first.

M Y D AY I S E NDING

Once again, Lord,
you have called me to think about
what I am striving for—
for myself, for my family,
for the community I live in.
You know well that I want to be happy
and to give others the means to be happy,
to be fulfilled and do something good for others.
I know these are good things
and that they are what almost everyone wants.
One need not be your disciple to strive for this.

What is the shape of the compassionate life
that I should strive for as your disciple?
How can I use the gifts and talents you have given me
not only to move up but to move down as well?
And how can I help those dear to me to do the same?
You have told me, "Anyone who loves his life loses it."
Help me to realize that my life is not my own,
but a gift you have entrusted to me
to do your will, to make your kingdom
of mercy, justice, and peace a reality.
Let me remember that
my family is not my own; they are yours.
My community is not my own; they are yours.
You have given them to me
and called me to help them live as you have lived,
with compassion and solidarity
with the poor and suffering.

I thank you, Lord, for all you have given me,
and all you have called me to be.

DAY 24

MY DAY BEGINS

When Jesus asks his friends James and John,
the sons of Zebedee,
"Can you drink the cup that I am going to drink?"
he poses the question that goes right to the heart
of my priesthood and my life as a human being. . . .
I still remember the day, a few years ago,
when the story in which Jesus raises that question
was read during the Eucharist.
It was 8:30 in the morning,
and about twenty members of the Daybreak
community were gathered
in the little basement chapel.
Suddenly the words "Can you drink the cup?"
pierced my heart like the sharp spear of a hunter.

I knew at that moment—as with a flash of insight—
that taking this question seriously
would radically change our lives.
It is the question that has the power
to crack open a hardened heart
and lay bare the tendons of the spiritual life.

"Can you drink the cup?
Can you empty it to the dregs?
Can you taste all the sorrows and joys?
Can you live your life to the full
whatever it will bring?"
I realized these were our questions.
(*Can You Drink the Cup?* pp. 22, 23)

All Through the Day

Can I drink the cup?

My Day Is Ending

When James and John asked Jesus,
"Can we sit at your right hand in glory?"
they didn't exactly get what Jesus was all about,
or where this road they were on was headed.
Jesus' response was not a yes or a no but a question:
"Can you drink the cup that I am going to drink?"

Like James and John,
I don't always get it either, Lord.
I expect my life to go well,
to work out right, to have its rewards.
But it doesn't always happen,
and sometimes it seems it doesn't happen at all.

The cup of my life is not always sweet or fulfilling;
sometimes it's bitter.
This bitter cup is the one you were given to drink,
Lord,
when you were rejected and your road led to Calvary.
And yet because you accepted this cup
and drank it to the end,
your life was given back to you.
You were raised up, full of new life, transformed.

Lord Jesus, when the cup I am given to drink
is not what I wanted, help me to trust in you,
to believe that you will drink the cup with me,
and you will use whatever it brings
for my good and your glory.

DAY 25

My Day Begins

"Can you drink the cup that I am going to drink?"
Jesus asked his friends.
They answered yes,
but had no idea what he was talking about.
Jesus' cup is the cup of sorrow,
not just his own sorrow
but the sorrow of the whole human race.
It is a cup full of physical, mental,
and spiritual anguish.
It is the cup of starvation, torture,
loneliness, rejection, abandonment,
and immense anguish. . . .

[But] in the midst of the sorrows is consolation,
in the midst of the darkness is light,
in the midst of the despair is hope,
in the midst of Babylon is a glimpse of Jerusalem,
and in the midst of the army of demons
is the consoling angel.
The cup of sorrow, inconceivable as it seems,
is also the cup of joy.

Only when we discover this in our own life
can we consider drinking it.
(*Can You Drink the Cup?* pp. 39, 43)

ALL THROUGH THE DAY

The cup of sorrow . . . is also the cup of joy.

MY DAY IS ENDING

Lord Jesus,
I recall your words,
"Unless a grain of wheat falls to the ground and dies,
it remains just a grain of wheat;
but if it dies, it produces much fruit" (Jn 12:24).
As I reflect on my life, I know this is true,
even though in the moment of sorrow
I cannot see beyond the pain I am in.
Teach me, dear Jesus, to trust you more.
Help me to believe that even from my deepest sorrow
you can produce hope, courage, strength,
and new life.
Let me drink the cup of sorrow to its dregs
and discover there the cup of joy.

Lord, I know that my sorrows are my own,
and that next to the pain and suffering in this world

they are small.
Help me to move through my own sorrows
to embrace the physical, mental, and spiritual sorrows
of all my brothers and sisters in this world,
those near to me,
and those whose lives will never intersect with mine.

Lord, may my share in your suffering
give me a share in your joy.

DAY 26

My Day Begins

Lifting our lives to others happens every time
we speak or act in ways that make our lives
lives for others.
When we are fully able to embrace our own lives,
we discover that what we claim
we also want to proclaim.
A life well held is indeed a life for others.
We stop wondering
whether our life is better or worse than others
and start seeing clearly
that when we live our life for others
we not only claim our individuality
but also proclaim our unique place
in the mosaic of the human family.

So often we are inclined to keep our lives hidden.
Shame and guilt prevent us
from letting others know what we are living. . . .
Lifting our cup means sharing our life
so we can celebrate it.
When we truly believe we are called
to lay down our lives for our friends,

we must dare to take the risk
to let others know what we are living.
(*Can You Drink the Cup?* pp. 64–65)

A L L   T H R O U G H   T H E   D A Y

I will make my life a life for others.

M Y   D A Y   I S   E N D I N G

Lord,
I know that each day of my life
is like another tile in a mosaic.
Today, like every day,
has had its share of joy and sorrow,
success and failure,
generosity and selfishness.
As this day ends, I take it in my hands
and offer it to you,
with gratitude and contrition.
I trust that you will make something beautiful
of my life.

As I have offered it to you, I ask you
to give me the humility and courage
to lift it up and offer it to others.
Do not let shame or guilt

make me afraid to share the life you have given me.
Help me to be open about my struggles and fears
and to believe that through them
someone else can find hope and strength.
Let me dare to take the risk
to let others know what I am living.
Let me trust you and believe
that you are creating a beautiful mosaic out of my life,
and an even richer and more beautiful one
when I share my life with others.

DAY 27

M y   D a y   B e g i n s

Here the mystery of drinking the cup becomes clear.
The coming and leaving of friends,
the experiences of love and betrayal,
of care and indifference, of generosity and stinginess
can become the way to true human freedom.
Yes, people who love us also disappoint us,
moments of great satisfaction also reveal
unfulfilled needs,
being home also shows us our homelessness.

But all of these tensions can create in us
that deep, deep yearning for full freedom
that is beyond any of the structures of our world.
Indeed, there is a mission emerging out of a life
that is never pure sorrow or pure joy,
a mission that makes us move far beyond
our human limitations
and reach out to total freedom,
complete redemption, ultimate salvation.
(*Can You Drink the Cup?* pp. 95–96)

ALL THROUGH THE DAY

My soul is longing for your peace.

MY DAY IS ENDING

Loving God,
when I reflect on the times in my life,
perhaps even in this day,
when joy and sorrow intersect,
my words fall short.
To say my life is bittersweet does not do it justice.
I know that even in the midst of my greatest joys,
there is something more that I am longing for.
And even in the depths of anguish,
there is something worth clinging to, hoping for.
This is the mystery at the heart of my life.
This is the illusive presence that you are.

You, O Lord, are in the poignant touch,
the heartrending embrace,
the distressing smile.
You are present in each moment
that leaves me full and yet longing,
empty yet open.

All of these tensions create in me
a deep, deep yearning
that only you can fill.
Help me, Lord,
to enter freely into that sacred space
where joy and sorrow meet,
that place where you dwell in mystery.

DAY 28

My Day Begins

In Jesus' agony we see the agony of the world
in all its gripping intensity:
"He began to feel sadness and anguish.
Then he said . . .
'My soul is sorrowful to the point of death'" (Mt
26:37–38).
Is not every human being
who wants to live with the mind of Christ
also called to die with the mind of Christ?
This can mean very different things
for different people. . . .
Yet it seems at least important to understand
that those who live with Christ
must also be prepared to die with him,
to be willing even to accept the invitation to enter into
his agony.

What then is this agony? . . .
I do not know, but if I have any sense of what I saw . . .
it was the fear of the great abyss which separates God
from us,
a distance which can only be bridged by faith.

The test comes when everything that is dear to us
slips away—
our home and those we love,
our body and its many ways of living,
our mind and its caring thoughts—
and there is absolutely nothing left to hold on to.
It is then that one must have the faith to surrender to a
loving Lord,
to believe that he will not allow us to fall
into a cruel and bottomless canyon,
but will bring us to the safe home which he has
prepared for us.
(*In Memoriam*, pp. 20–21)

All Through the Day

Into your hands, Lord, I commend my spirit.

My Day Is Ending

Lord Jesus,
even before I was conceived
you knew me and loved me.
I believe that your tender care has sustained me
through every moment of my life,
and that you will continue to lead and guide me
through the days that remain to me.

I trust that just as I have tried to live with you,
when the hour of my death comes,
so too will I die with you.

And yet, Lord, you know that I sometimes fear death.
Like Peter who stepped out of the boat to walk to you
on water
I feel myself sinking and cry out,
"Lord, save me!"
I give this fear to you, Lord Jesus.
Give me the confidence to trust you
and believe that you will not allow me
to fall into a cruel and bottomless abyss
but will bring me safely home
to the place you have prepared for me.

DAY 29

My Day Begins

When God himself in his humanity
became part of our most painful experience
of God's absence,
he became most present to us.
It is into this mystery that we enter when we pray.
The intimacy with God in our earthly existence
will always remain an intimacy
that transcends human intimacy
and is experienced in a faithful waiting on him
who came but is still to come.
Although at exceptional moments
we may be overwhelmed by a deep sense
of God's presence
in the center of our solitude
and in the midst of the space we create for others,
more often than not we are left
with the painful sense of emptiness
and can only experience God as the absent God. . . .

The mystery of God's presence, therefore,
can be touched only by a deep
awareness of his absence.

It is in the center of our longing for the absent God
that we discover his footprints
and realize that our desire to love God
is born out of the love with which he has touched us.
In the patient waiting for the loved one
we discover how much he has filled our lives already.
(*Reaching Out*, p. 91)

ALL THROUGH THE DAY

I will wait patiently.

MY DAY IS ENDING

I wonder, Lord,
what your disciples were thinking and feeling
on that first Saturday after you died,
before you rose.
"We were hoping that he would be the one . . ."
two of them said as they walked with a stranger
on the road to Emmaus.
Remembering you,
we anguish about how this could be,
losing hope.
And yet we call that day Holy Saturday
because we know that your death, your absence,

was not the end of the story
and that the waiting is itself sacred.

Lord, help me remember
in the times when I cannot find you,
that though you died and were absent for a moment,
you rose and are living still.
Help me to accept that
the mystery of you presence
can be touched only by a deep awareness
of your absence.

DAY 30

My Day Begins

To live in the present we must believe deeply
that what is most important is the here and now.
We are constantly distracted
by things that have happened in the past
or that might happen in the future.
It is not easy to remain focused on the present.

Our mind is hard to master
and keeps pulling us away from the moment.
Prayer is the discipline of the moment.
When we pray we enter into the presence of God
whose name is God-with-us.
To pray is to listen attentively
to the one who addresses us here and now.

When we dare to trust that we are never alone
but that God is always with us,
always cares for us, and always speaks to us,
then we can gradually detach ourselves
from the voices that make us guilty or anxious
and thus allow ourselves to dwell
in the present moment.

This is a very hard challenge
because radical trust in God is not obvious.
Most of us distrust God.
Most of us think of God as a fearful, punitive authority
or as an empty powerless nothing.
Jesus' core message was that
God is neither a powerless weakling
nor a powerful boss,
but a lover
whose only desire is to give us
what our hearts most desire.
(*Here and Now*, pp. 19–20)

A L L   T H R O U G H   T H E   D A Y

God is here. God is now.

M Y   D A Y   I S   E N D I N G

Lord, you know me well,
how my mind is always working,
jumping to and fro like a monkey in a tree.
Stillness is so hard for me.
Keep me faithful in prayer.
Teach me not to measure its worth
by how well I master my mind.

Give me the wisdom not to dwell on the past
with its failures or regrets.
Give me the hope not to worry about the future
for I cannot control it.
Give me your peace to live in this moment.
For all that has been, I thank you.
For all that will be, I trust you.
For all that is, I say yes.
Let me see the beauty that surrounds me,
in this world that you have made,
in the people you have given me,
and in my very self,
whom you love and cherish.

Gracious God,
I thank you for your servant Henri Nouwen,
and for these thirty days when you have used his
words
to teach and guide me.
Help me to imitate his fidelity to you
and his faithfulness.
Help me, as he did, to encourage others
in their spiritual lives
by learning to share my own joys and struggles.

You have been with me Lord, each day of my past,
you will stay with me every day of the future,
you are with me here, and
you are with me now.
Amen.

ONE FINAL WORD

This book was created to be nothing more than a gateway—a gateway to the spiritual wisdom of a specific teacher and a gateway opening on your own spiritual way.

You may decide that Henri Nouwen is someone whose experience of God is one that you wish to follow more closely and deeply, in which case you should get a copy of one of the books quoted in this text and pray it as you have prayed this gateway journey.

You may decide that his experience has not helped you. There are many other teachers. Somewhere there is the right teacher for your own, very special, absolutely unique journey of the spirit. You will find your teacher. You will discover your path.

We would not be searching, as St. Augustine reminds us, if we had not already been found.

NOTES

1. "About Henri," Henri Nouwen Society, accessed May 3, 2019, https://HenriNouwen.org.

2. "Who Was Henri Nouwen?" Henri Nouwen Society, accessed May 3, 2019, https://HenriNouwen.org.

3. Henri J. M. Nouwen, *A Letter of Consolation* (San Francisco: Harper and Row, 1982), 63.

4. Henri J. M. Nouwen, *Behold the Beauty of the Lord* (Notre Dame, IN: Ave Maria Press, 1987, 2007), 20.

5. Quoted by Thomas Petriano, "Henri, Rembrandt, and Vincent," in *Remembering Henri*, ed. Gerald S. Toomey and Claude Pomerleau (Maryknoll, NY: Orbis Books, 2006), 110.

6. Henri J. M. Nouwen, *The Return of the Prodigal Son* (New York: Doubleday, 1992), 8.

7. Nouwen, *Return of the Prodigal Son*, 133.

PERMISSIONS

All the scripture quotes in the various pieces are intact: some are drawn from translations used in the twentieth century such as the New Jerusalem Bible, while others synthesize pieces of multiple translations—likely Nouwen was quoting from memory or making his own translations into English.

Ave Maria Press is grateful to the publishers who have allowed excerpts from Nouwen works to be included in this book. Prayers in this book are also excerpted from the following texts published by other houses:

Here and Now by Nouwen, Henri J. M. (Crossroad, 2006). Reprinted by arrangement with The Crossroad Publishing Company. www.crossroadpublishing.com Copyright © Nouwen, Henri J. M.

Life of the Beloved by Nouwen, Henri J. M. (Crossroad, 2002). Reprinted by arrangement with The Crossroad Publishing Company. www.crossroadpublishing. com Copyright © Nouwen, Henri J. M.

Reaching Out: The Three Movements of the Spiritual Life by Henri Nouwen, copyright ©1975 by Henri J. M. Nouwen. Copyright renewed ©2003 by Sue Mosteller, Executor of the Estate of Henri J. M. Nouwen. Used by permission of Doubleday, an imprint of the Knopf